The Magpie's Box

Terry Simpson

ISBN: 978-1-913122-01-0

Cover image: © Copyright Joanna Sedgwick

Cover design: Lorna Faye Dunsire

Typesetting: Mike Farren

Acknowledgements

Several poems were first published in the following journals and anthologies:
'In praise of water' in *Scattered Leaves: the magazine of the Living Artists Movement*; 'Did those feet walk in Woodhouse' in Aireings magazine; 'Staincross', 'Resplendent' and 'Mr. Nock' in *Check Hope Remains: poems from Rommi Smith's Poetry Workshop*, (125th & Midnight); 'Luis' in *Gathered Leaves: an anthology of the Living Artists Movement*; 'The band' in *River of Voices: a chapbook by the Mouth of the River collective*; 'The offbeat' in the 100 thousand poets for change (100 TPC) online anthology (2017); 'Rubbish' won the 2001 Martha Robinson Poetry Competition.

Thanks to Rommi Smith and members of her Poetry Workshop over the years, where many of these poems first saw the light of day.

The Magpie's Box was a 1977 installation by the British artist Rose Finn-Kelcey.

Contents

For Joyce Simpson:
A Cumberland lass,
without whom this collection
would not have been possible

Joy

Two out for trouble in the pale afternoon,
cockily bounce, pick at daisies,
matt heads so dense light daren't go there.

They keep a wary eye on Rampart Road,
where trader's vans and bunking students
pass too fast. They don't take a chance

on a sudden ginger dog, wafting up like shreds
of bin bag to the blighted sycamore,
biding time, checking out the scene

by Merano's Pizza's, casing Nazam's
and The Seven Spices, scanning the grass
for limp pakora, burgers in a bun.

Bright survivors' eyes miss nothing.
They know for a scavenger death is never far,
but there's always treasure in the Woodhouse trash –

dismembered quattro formaggio crusts;
spattered entrails of weathered noodles;
hard white rice, old water chestnuts.

Later the fox and the rat will come,
but for now these two are cleaning up,
ruling the roost, winding up the dogs
with their football rattle warnings.

Staincross

This Summer
rosebay platforms are our playground,
channelling bright rails on which a goods train hisses,
impatient, held by a signal at the bridge –
where my blond-angel brother calls the crew,
and we're beckoned to the hot cab,
to watch the fireman in oily blue
shovel blocks of shiny coal into the boiler,
and in the white canyons of a Black Five's belly
I see my first glimpse of Hell.

That's when your heartaches begin

Music invented me in Grandma's kitchen
through a box of wood and valves,
invoking the mystery of 'BFPO'.
"Where will the baby's dimple be?"

I followed where it led as best I could, through
"Hills of the North" rejoicing in the parqueted hall
of Mapplewell County Primary, imagining
"inch-worms and marigolds" on heaps of slag,

through jumble sale 78s to Luxembourg,
under the blankets on a Sunday evening;
visions of America among the pop bottles.
"Muddy River, you took my baby's life".

My father gave abrupt directions,
adopting for no good reason a plantation accent.
"The folks up North will see me no more",
my suggestion for his gravestone.

Garforth Cliff (circa 1957)

A bit of a wide boy, known as a singer
down the Ring o' Bells; a pit-village Bogart
with centre-parted Brylcreem hair,
a winning smile, a flare for risqué chat.

With whining kids it's "don't get me started",
growling behind the News of the Screws;
words backed by threat of the back of a hand,
or front if wrestling's on, or news.

Later you'll be singing '*Mammy*' in the kitchen,
practising aeroplane spins on the children.

Elders

We boil tiny grapes on granma's fire,
in the shiny range where rags of towel dry.
The old deaf lodger spits and misses. All afternoon
a clot of spittle dangles from a vest. Either no-one
sees, or pretends they don't. Later we bleed
berry pulp through pale muslin stretched
across an upturned chair. I'm sent to fetch
more from the bedroom where the dead
moulting fox straddles a glass eyed bunny.
We add white sugar. She gives me a mug.
"Drink. It won't hurt you. It'll do you good."
And his wheezing echo, "yes, lad, do you good."

Resplendent

I don't know where I found the word –
not home surely, or in the prefab class
of our mill town with its black stone hall.
But when, age ten, I had to describe
my summer, it rose up like a genie,
conjuring a steam train, the polished olive,
tapered boiler of a Great Western 'King',
and no other word could say that spell.
I wrote it on the white page, wondering
at the simple power of it, and smelt that King again;
heard the threat of its whistle rip the sky,
transported to that sunlit platform,
my parents still not old, still almost carefree,
and the wonder of the word come alive in me.

Mr. Nock

meant well, and didn't need to shout;
was big with dignity, the brains behind the Head,
it seemed to me. He wore round specs, and didn't clout,

but said regretful words instead,
in sad and disappointed tones when we were bad.
He refereed our muddy games, and sensed my dread

of the dirty tackle on Churwell Hill. He had
no bones about sons of millworkers' wives,
in this town where looms deafened the dads

of boys who sold me Columbia 45's
after youth club, as we gobbled scraps and chips.
He saw a spark in our foggy lives,

and one day with new blue suit, tight lips,
he stood in our front room, articulate, refined,
and said that I should sit a scholarship.

So the world opened up a path for my mind,
and I stepped forward, no question or doubt.
That great future ahead, that door slammed shut behind.

The scholarship of Icarus

Now you must give humble and hearty thanks
      for the opportunity laid before you
take these feathers and wax

That you may become a profitable member
      of Church and Commonwealth
you have been spared mine and mill

That you may be a partaker of the immortal glory
      of the Resurrection
you have been summoned from the slum

Beseech our most merciful Father for grace
      to use his blessings
don't fly close to the sea, less it dampen your wings

Answer the good intent of our religious founders
aim for the sun.

Pentecostal

After reading again the first page of 'Free Fall' *by William Golding*

When you walked by those market stalls,
     William, it was something I'd always known.

Those fading purple, dog-eared books bursting white
     with hosanna, more alive than people;

your double-crowned crook and flail, power and glory,
     lifting me to dream among council tower blocks.

I understood how scar turns star, how flakes of fire fall
     on the hunger of a scholarship boy.

Now my own yesterdays run beside, outpacing me.
     I'm ready to turn and look into the eyes

of faces peering over my shoulder,
     seeing them, as if for the first time,

                      miraculous

Luis

He feeds the pigeons and the cats,
keeps them apart,
brings the wheelies back
from down the hill where the kids ride them.
His Spanish gets louder the more he drinks.
Every passer on Christopher Road gets a shout,
while from his open door salsa parties out,
or Jim Reeves sings *"I won't forget you"*.
He films misdeeds of the young men who bait him,
but still lets them sell him malfunctioning mobiles.
He told me once he played football against Pelé
for Chile, before the coup and exile.
He hasn't slept well since they fractured his skull.
I believed him about Pelé,
but later after more White Lightning,
he also claimed an affair with
Dame Judi Dench.

Spring-time in Woodhouse

My student neighbours
smoke weed on the doorstep and smile.
They are dilated to see me,
(though they don't seem sure
they've seen me before). "Hi man."

It's Spring-time in Woodhouse.
Black steel security grilles
are thrown open to sunlight.
A woman batters on a door
"Let me in you bastard!"
OK to lock people out
now the temperature's gone up.

It's Spring-time in Woodhouse.
Kids play footy on terraced streets
of a thousand windows,
where car alarms erupt in spontaneous joy.
On Woodhouse Moor dogs shit in the sun,
no need to crouch and cower against the weather,
today they can be proud.

It's Spring-time in Woodhouse.
The post office is selling beer,
the off-licence stamps,
the corner shop sells balloons
and paraffin lamps.

Its spring-time in Woodhouse
what can you say?
The sun has got his giro
hip hip, hip hip hooray,
the sun has got his giro
and he's coming out to play

Rubbish

I devote the morning to waste,
lugging a month's vegetable gatherings
to Hannah's heap,
crushing cartons and steel cans in her cellar,
separating aluminium wheat with a magnet.

There's resistance
from jagged steel edges with rust for defence,
and the uncleaned plastic
is rancid with old milk.
I am happy with a peasant's slow pleasure
watching order appear.

I am a minor miracle
risen from the dead, recycled,
each slow heartbeat of a day
more than they could have predicted
or I could expect.

I tend this waste
where nothing is too small to notice or consider,
accept, reject, grade, gather and harvest.
I rejoice in the world's debris,
rubbish reborn
to hold the world
in a new form.

Did those feet walk in Woodhouse?

They come early morning down Quarry Street,
smashing both cars and downstairs windows
at the dealers' place. Next day a van comes,
and the broken house is empty for a month.

But May on the corner talks to everyone
on daily walks with her reluctant terrier,
plants her tubs, a blue chimney pot,
and they never get trashed.

Luis feeds the pigeons and scrawny cats,
advising on security, and bad boys' moves,
one day heaves a couch to my front door –
"I thought you'd like it, I found it in a binyard".

In Hannah's alley there are condoms and glass,
but this year, finally, she wins Leeds In Bloom
'urban class', with her night-scented stocks,
her blind cat sleeping under the honeysuckle.

Every day gaudy leaflets are delivered,
for pizzas and kebabs, through black grilles
of back-to-backs. But Sophie and Esther
put their sofa in the street,
          and read in the sunshine all weekend.

In praise of water

She remembers chaos, time before
there was a when, or human eye to see;
reflects back on our mortal world
from pond or puddle, this road sign, that tree.

We capture her, and she agrees to sit
in reservoir, straight glass or cooler;
listening with no comment to our gossip,
noticing our sweat or how we drool.

Rumour is she invented life –
mist, storm and wave not flexible enough
to roam the world as she would like,

so she appears in buddleia, convolvulus,
that rosebay blooming in the dirt,
this cloud of humans fretting over words.

The band

You have assembled in the old hall,
commented on the chill, set up your stands
of ancient, skeletal steel, or new and varnished wood;
tuned strings to a veteran piano's pitch;
watched dancers enter; cracked old jokes –
"from each accordion to his abilities."

The leader exudes hope,
hands out paper,
on which dots cluster
like captured insects
ready for flight.
He shakes his white mane,
calls for order.

      The first tentative notes
explore the cold. You play the solid blocks of chords, building
a foundation fiddlers can weave a sky above,
for you are merely rhythm, but they are melody.

      And at first the dancers pull the tune along.
Journeyman players reach above themselves,
labouring for time and for each other,
and then from nowhere

that unexpected lift,
      hoisting dancers and players together,
like some sea beast that rises from the waters
           to carry you all forward on its back,
and you can only wonder where it came from?
           where it will take you?
and who you will be when you arrive?

The offbeat

You taught me how to hit it,
that beat that cuts the solid four
and gives the tune a catch fiddlers can play to.
You taught me how to play
that upward, backward strum against the grain.

Playing on the beat is safe –
the machine beat, safe rock 'n' roll (2-3-4)
"**here** we are and **here** we are and **here** we go";
it's the fascist march
"**Fatherland, Fatherland, Show** us a **Sign**."

Playing off the beat outraged the ears
of the musical elite –
"c'mon and hear, c'mon and hear,
Alexander's Ragtime Band"
The syncopation an invitation to emancipation.

Playing off the beat is the possibility of dance –
"step **we gaily** on **we** go, heel **for** heel **and** toe **for** toe
arm **in** arm **and** row **on** row, all **for** Mairi's wedding".

It's the offbeat beat that makes the beat
that makes you want to tap your feet, that makes the heat.

Martin Luther King suggested
all progress depends on the maladjusted.
If you're happy with the way of it
you've got no reason to shout.
It's the maladjusted who've got the frustration
and the motivation to make the change.
It's the maladjusted will sort this sad world out.

So don't be afraid to step out of line,
and be a lone voice, be out of time,

saying the true thing orthodoxy needs to put it right
and make it rhyme.

The beat needs the offbeat
like the sour needs the sweet, or the cold the heat.

We should welcome the strange, and the danger it brings
and the way it rearranges things.

We should welcome the wilderness and the way it sings in us,
and the brilliant things it brings to us.

We should welcome the offbeat.
In a world that's dancing to the beat
of a corporate elite,
                        we are the offbeat.

The midsummer wedding party

His dead brother wasn't invited, so it was a surprise
to see him walk in with tache and tattoos.
The hall was given over to pagan rites,
its wooden plainness transformed by women,
garlanded in green with sweet star of hellebore,
forget-me-nots for enduring love.
Invisible to other eyes, his brother plucked a rose,
sniffed it, grimaced and threw it over his shoulder.
It was almost too hot to dance.
Boys in suits angled for a drink
at the trestle table, where a tipsy uncle
with Charlton comb-over inclined to generosity.
The band played "another bride, another June",
while the caller in pink straw hat sorted relatives:
"I want four sets of four, don't be shy".
His brother ignored her, put down his plastic pint,
rolling a fag under the "no smoking" sign.
The bride was saying they'd gone to the hills
after the registry, to where her dad was buried;
she like a hyacinth, blooming pink;
the quiet groom tall and Irish.
Red-faced aunts couldn't stop laughing,
opening the windows so the heavy smell
of hay and moor surged in with the warmth.
The band played a jig and the best man fell over.
The earnest musician caught his brother
appraising a bridesmaid, winking back at him.
He saw the caller's animated shadow,
on the wall's panels, commanding dancers,
ribbons flying, broad-brimmed hat
emphatic, arms like branches in a squall;
and the church hall was a cave, and the music a fire,

and them in their dance as the wheel turned,
even his brother tapping his feet.

The birth of Magpie

Crow with raucous voice ruled
other birds with harsh devotion,
but growing old, worried his boys
were too weak, he made a potion,
took three pints of brackish Swinsty lake,
threw in clumps of wool from Pennine wire,
coal from Ribblehead viaduct,
lime from caves deep under the moor.
Whoever drank this brew would be cunning,
tenacious and bold, a mighty warrior.
He put the white dove, noted for obedience
to watch the bubbling pot.

Pure as milk and mild as Ilkley,
Dove was dozing when a droplet
flew out from the viscous liquid.
Without thinking he sipped it up,
then with sudden vision knew his fate.
Terror filled his little frame,
and off he flew.

When Crow found out he was furious,
searched and found Dove outside Londis,
beat him black and blue and bloody.
But with new powers Dove twisted away,
and turned into a Triumph Norton,
screeching down Sheepscar like a banshee.
But Crow became a Harley Roadster
quickly caught him by The Primrose.

So Dove turned into a Ford Mondeo
and headed up to Hyde Park Corner.
But Crow became a Vauxhall Astra,
and quickly caught him, rammed him, stopped him.

Now this being Woodhouse there were heaps
of greasy takeaways,
vile decaying student throwaways,
banked in rancid piles in shop doorways,
and Dove became a half-eaten bag of chips,
and hid himself among the debris.
So Crow became a hungry student fox
and ate the whole lot, packaging and all,
and thought he'd killed the lowly pigeon.

But that night he dreamt a brooding dream
of an awful scavenging blue black bird,
with a terrible cry. He woke in fear
but just when reassured
his brain split open and out emerged
Magpie as from a mother's egg,
brain and membrane oozing from his wings,
as he shook the night, announcing his arrival.

When Magpie was up for an award

Magpie was nominated in a competition
to find a bird to symbolise our nation.
The four finalists entered, and there was a silence,
as the Great Man introduced them to the TV audience.

Owl, he said, your wisdom is renowned
from coast to coast and town to town.
Your sagacity and thoughtfulness
are beyond doubt, we're most impressed.
You're a brilliant hunter, we like your dulcet tones,
that little trick you do when you spit out the bones.

Hawk, your fearlessness is proved.
You're second to none, we're very moved
by the viral YouTube highlights
of your recent brilliant fights.
We're amazed by your perfect vision,
and the way you kill was made for television.

Sparrow, plucky little bird,
withstanding hardship, never deterred,
you don't complain about austerity,
you sing all day, happy in your tree,
accepting poverty as your lot,
you make the most of what you've got.

Magpie, you are selfish, vain,
you steal and lie, then cheat again,
always on the make it seems,
robbing others of their dreams.
Your face is brass, your heart is cold,
you rob the sick, the poor, the old.
You're violent, dirty, you just don't care,
you'll make a profit anywhere.

So it will come as no surprise
which bird we've chosen in our competition,
to sum up the qualities of our great nation –
Magpie, step forward and take your prize.

Magpie learns to sing

Magpie had been chosen to represent the nation,
but his voice was a terrible squawking,
a mechanical music
an electronic music
a digital music,
not at all like the sweet song birds.
This won't do, the singing-masters said.
They taped his ugly pecker shut
locked him in a darkened room,
played constant loops of white noise,
fed him at inconsistent times,
and when at last his eyes were blasted empty,
when his voice was gone completely,
played him tapes of blackbird and nightingale,
song thrush and linnet, all day long.

And so Magpie was trained to sing
the glory of the Lord's creation,
each little flower that knows its station,
all things bright and nothing mean,
and at last came to sing before the Queen.

And when the people gathered round
and silence hushed the mighty crowd,
anticipation ran through the throng,
Magpie opened his beak to start the song.

Such a terrible, raucous stammering,
such a dreadful, devilish clammering,
such an ugly, chattering yammering,
as Magpie attack-ack-ack-ack-acked the air
as if a crack-ack-ack was torn
in the black-ack-ackness of the formless void,
and people ran for cover.

It sounded like an air raid.
It sounded like Armageddon.
It sounded like all the spirits of hell
had escaped and were flying overhead.
The Queen retreated to her bed,
and Magpie was driven from the court by the Prince,
and has been a scavenger ever since.

Magpie takes a stand

Magpie was upset to find
his image used by a corporation.
Apparently his qualities typified
the virtues needed for their operation.
Asset-stripping, adventure capital,
buccaneering innovators,
buying cheap, selling fast,
ruthless sharp-eyed 'wealth creators',
they thought the brand of 'Magpie'
summarised their mission.
Their mistake was not requesting permission,
not cutting Magpie in on the deal.
They underestimated how he'd feel,
or didn't even consider,
used to only noticing the highest bidder.

Magpie landed at their reception
livid at this deception.
"You'll have to make an appointment,"
the receptionist said,
then made some wrenching, slicing sounds
as Magpie clawed off her head.
He flew up the stairwell,
seventeen storeys he mounted,
gouging out the eyes of those he encountered,
crashed through the glass door
like the harbinger of doom
he was, filled the boardroom with his vindictive caws
and claws, and paused only to note
terror in the chairman's eyes as he pecked out his throat.

Leaving the board gored and slaughtered on the floor
Magpie exulted, and ecstatic, exited.

He was happy to kill for no reason at all,
but he liked an excuse truth to tell
It whetted his appetite for a lark
and it being a home Saturday,
he headed for St. James's Park.